DRAW THE WORLD
AN OUTLINE OF CONTINENTS AND OCEANS

AN EASY STEP-BY-STEP APPROACH

BY
Kristin J. Draeger

Copyright 2017 by Kristin J. Draeger

All rights reserved. No part of this book may be reproduced, stored in a retrieval system, or transmitted in any form or by any means, electronic, mechanical, photocopying, recording, or otherwise, without the prior written permission of Kristin J. Draeger.

All of the maps in this book were drawn by Kristin J. Draeger and are copyrighted by Kristin J. Draeger ©2017. The majority of the tiny buildings on the cover and interior pages were drawn by Marina Zlochin ©2017.

ArtK12.com
info@artk12.com

Instructions

The Map

There are several models for dividing the world into continents. In this book we will use the traditional model that divides the land masses into seven continents: North America, South America, Africa, Europe, Asia, Australia and Antarctica. We will also label the five major world oceans: the Atlantic, Pacific, Arctic, Indian and Southern Oceans.

Because this is an outline, many, many details (including lakes, peninsulas, inlets, islands, and even some tiny countries) have been omitted. The goal of this book is to give students a basic outline of the world and to keep it simple enough that they can commit it to memory.

The Drawing

For this drawing use an 11x17 ledger-sized piece of paper or two 8 1/2x11 pieces of paper taped together (more instructions follow on pages 6-8). Follow the instructions in red, page-by-page, until the end of the book is reached. Unlike the other books in this series, the continents and oceans will be labeled at the end.

The map can be drawn all at once, but students may find it easier to master smaller portions of the map at a time. After drawing a portion of the map students may want to pause and practice what they have learned.

Coloring

If the student wishes to color the map, I recommend first inking it with a thin, black, permanent marker. This will help maintain the integrity of the outline and give the final product a more "professional" look.

Enjoy.

For Camp Draeger: Seth, Jesse, Jenna, Ryan, Hannah, Caroline, Caleb, Jaella, Brennan and Jennifer.

PAPER

Before you begin to draw your map of the world you will need to prepare your paper. If you have an 11x17 ledger-sized piece of paper, yahoo! You are ready to go. If not, never fear! You can easily make one by taping two 8 1/2x11 sized pieces of paper together as shown below (the yellow line is the tape).

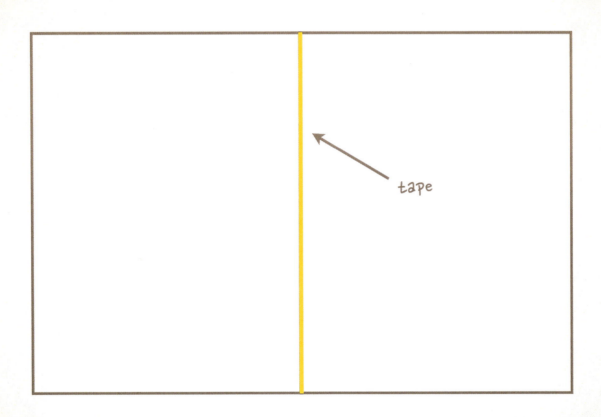

tape

Now fold your large piece of paper two times the short way, and one time the long way. (If you taped two pieces of paper together the center fold will be your taped joint.)

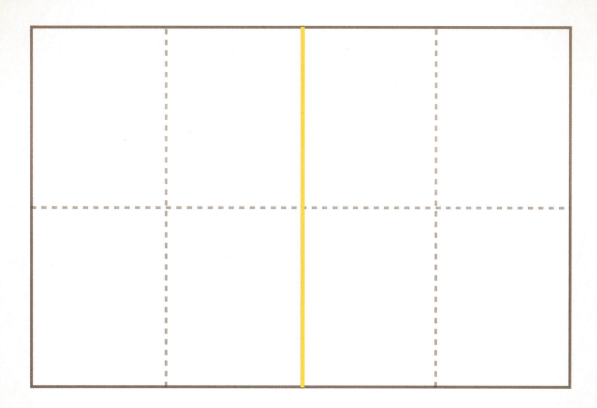

PAPER

Now take a yellow crayon, marker or colored pencil and trace the vertical center fold line. This will help you locate where you are on the paper. Next trace the horizontal fold line with something green. This is the equator.

Ba-da-bing! We are ready to rock and roll!

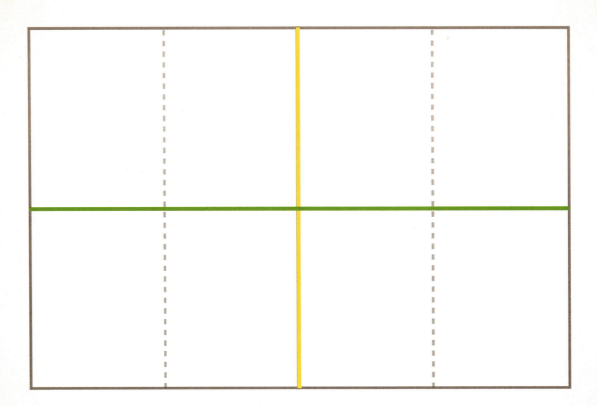

SOUTH AMERICA

gap

To position North America in the correct place, we will first draw the northwest corner of South America. Notice that there is a gap where North America will connect.

NORTH AMERICA

imaginary halfway mark

Now we will add a hook and a squiggly line (those are technical terms) that will eventually look like the southeastern coast of North America. Notice that both of these lines are below the imaginary halfway mark on this quarter of the paper.

NORTH AMERICA

imaginary halfway mark

Cuba
Hispaniola

Connect the two lines with a "c," add the islands of Cuba and Hispaniola* and we have the Gulf of Mexico and the Caribbean Sea.

*Yep, there are waaaay more than two islands in the Caribbean, but remember, this is a simplified version of the world.

NORTH AMERICA

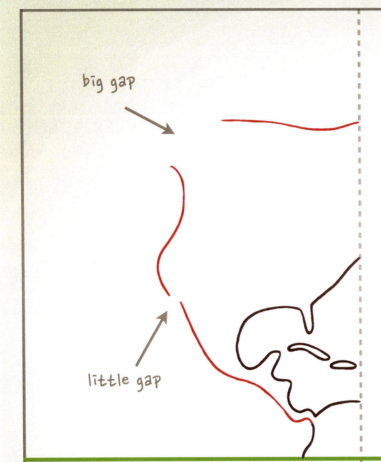

Now draw the basic outline of the continent like so. Leave a little gap and a big gap!

NORTH AMERICA

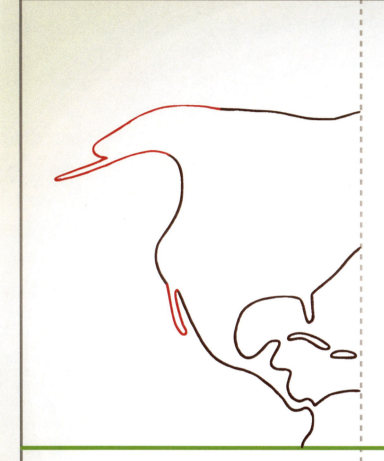

Fill in the big gap with the state of Alaska (that looks a little like an elephant's head), and fill in the little gap with Baja California. This peninsula makes North America look like it has a tail.

NORTH AMERICA

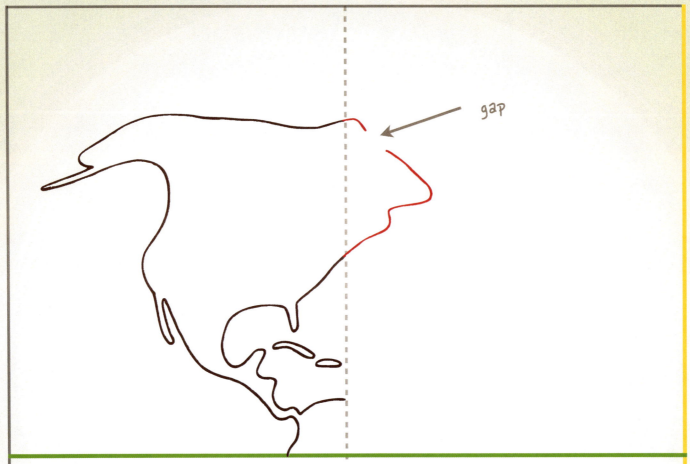

gap

As we draw the northern areas of Canada you will notice that we are simplifying tremendously. Canada is a very complicated country. Fortunately it is also a very forgiving country and won't mind if we leave out some details.

NORTH AMERICA

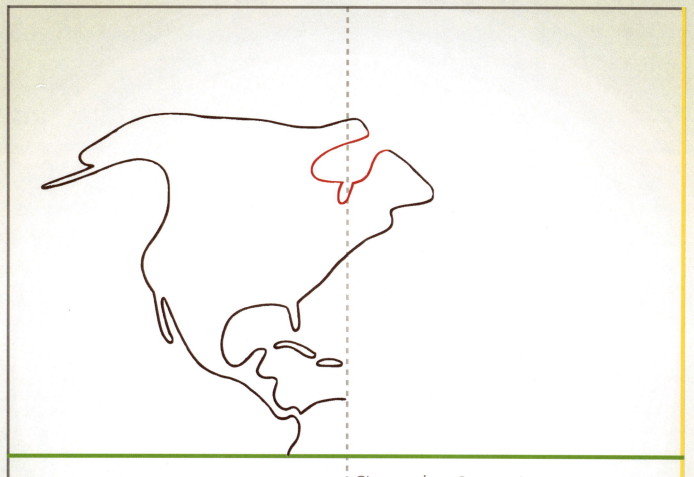

Place Hudson Bay in the gap.

NORTH AMERICA

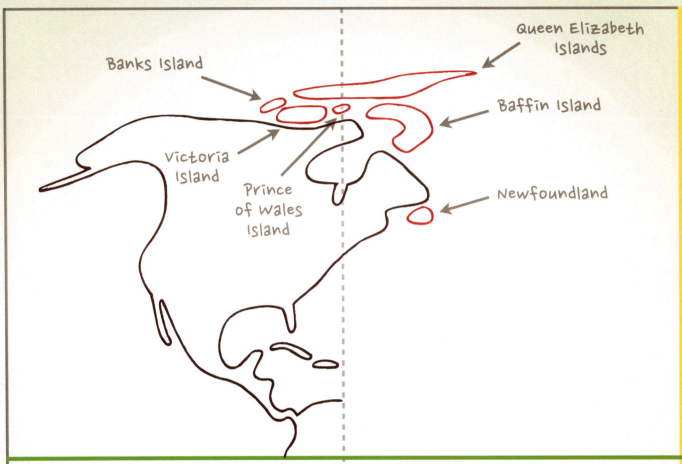

Canada has many, many, many islands, but for the sake of simplicity we are only drawing six. The large island on the top represents a group of islands called the Queen Elizabeth Islands. Below this group, from left to right, are: Banks Island, Victoria Island, Prince of Wales Island and Baffin Island. The southernmost island is Newfoundland.

NORTH AMERICA

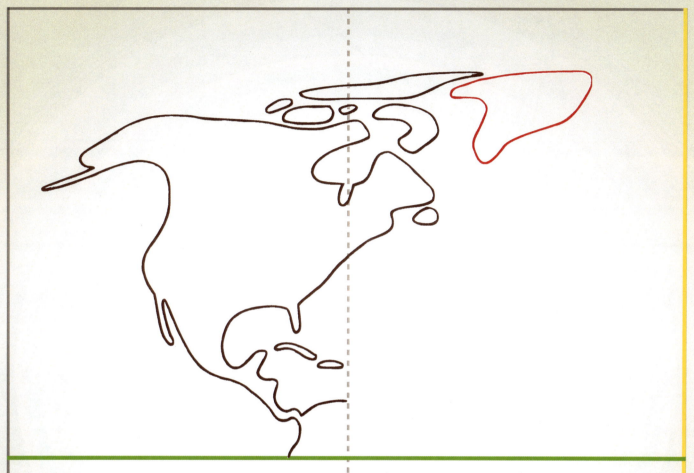

Don't forget Greenland! Notice how close it is to the Queen Elizabeth Islands.

SOUTH AMERICA

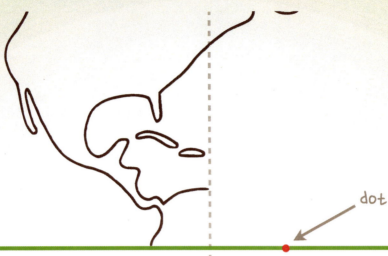

dot

dot

imaginary halfway mark

Now we will return to South America. Place these two dots. Notice that the southernmost dot is just about at the imaginary halfway mark.

SOUTH AMERICA

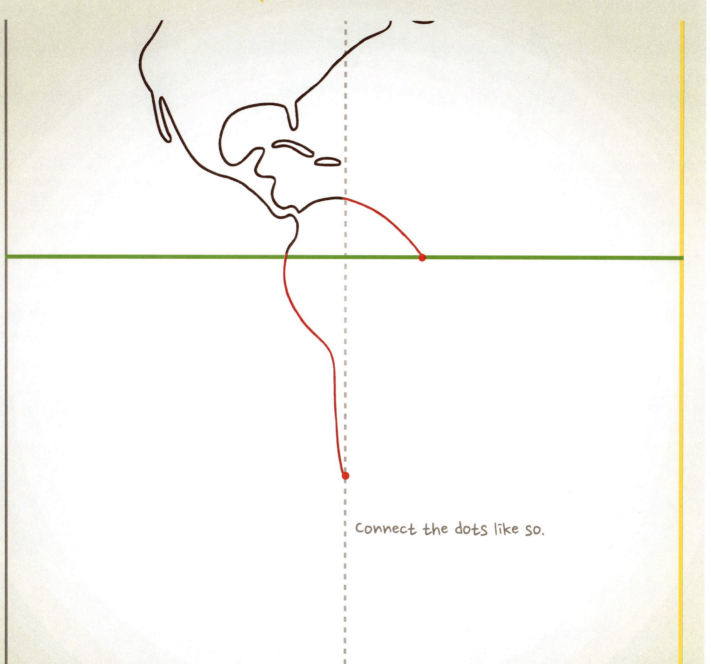

Connect the dots like so.

SOUTH AMERICA

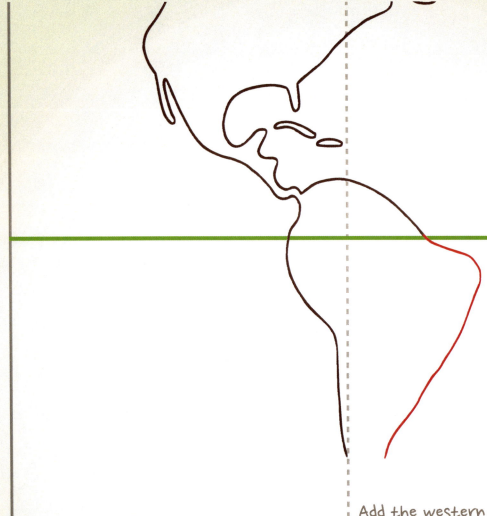

Add the western shore.

SOUTH AMERICA

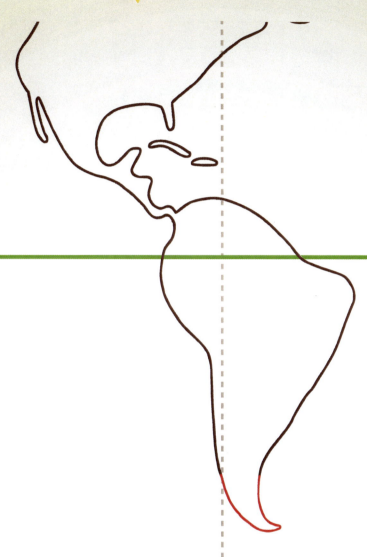

And then finish with a hook-like thingy (technically called Tierra del Fuego).

EUROPE

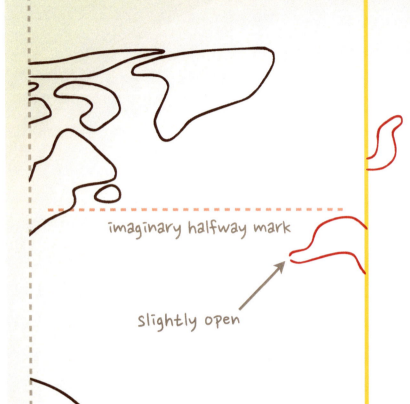

imaginary halfway mark

slightly open

On to the center of the page! Europe is tricky; we will begin with two shapes. First draw a slug-like shape slithering east of the yellow line (this is the Baltic Sea). Then a duck head facing west of the yellow line (this will be part of the Mediterranean Sea). Notice that the duck head is just below the imaginary halfway mark, AND his beak is slightly open - very important.

EUROPE

Connect the bottom of the slug to the top of the duck's beak with this shape. Can you recognize Denmark, France and Spain?

EUROPE

Iceland
Great Britain
Ireland

Add three islands: Iceland, Ireland and Great Britain.

EUROPE

dot →

Add this shape to continue outlining northern Europe. Then add a dot.

EUROPE

gap

Connect the bit of Norway on the yellow line to the dot. This is the northern shore of Norway and Russia. And as they say in England: mind the gap!

EUROPE

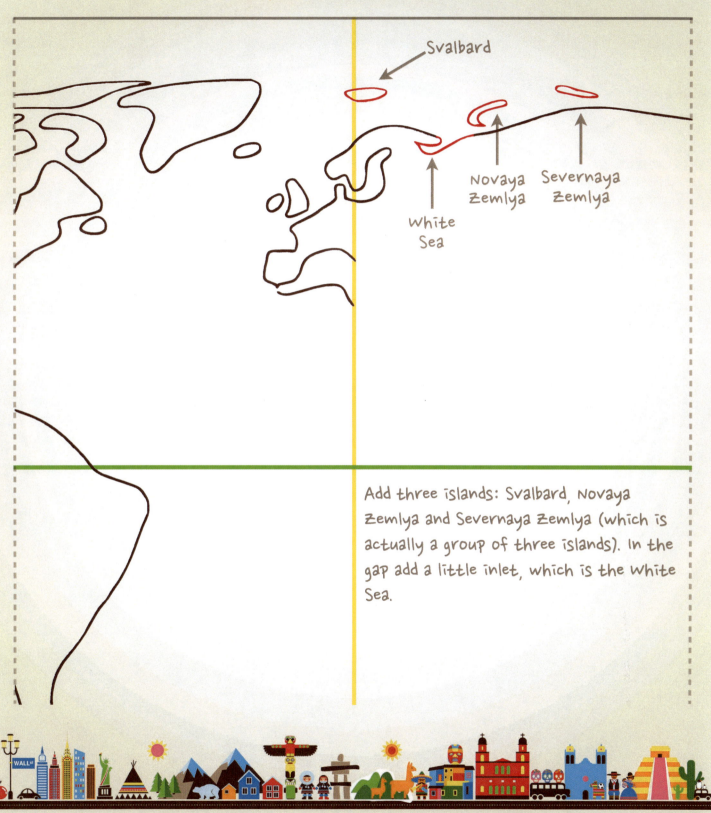

Add three islands: Svalbard, Novaya Zemlya and Severnaya Zemlya (which is actually a group of three islands). In the gap add a little inlet, which is the White Sea.

EUROPE

little hook

Back to the duck. Give him a body and a little hook behind his head. The hook is very important; it's Italy, and if you forget it they will be very put out.

EUROPE

Now give the duck two wings: a tall skinny one, and a shorter, fat one. Step back and take a look. Your duck is the Mediterranean sea. Can you see Italy and Greece?

EUROPE

Behind the duck are the Black Sea and the Caspian Sea.

AFRICA

← dot

On to Africa! Begin drawing Africa by carefully placing this dot.

AFRICA

dot

imaginary halfway mark

Connect the bottom of the duck's beak to the dot like so. Then add another dot. Notice that this dot is above the imaginary halfway mark on this quarter of the page.

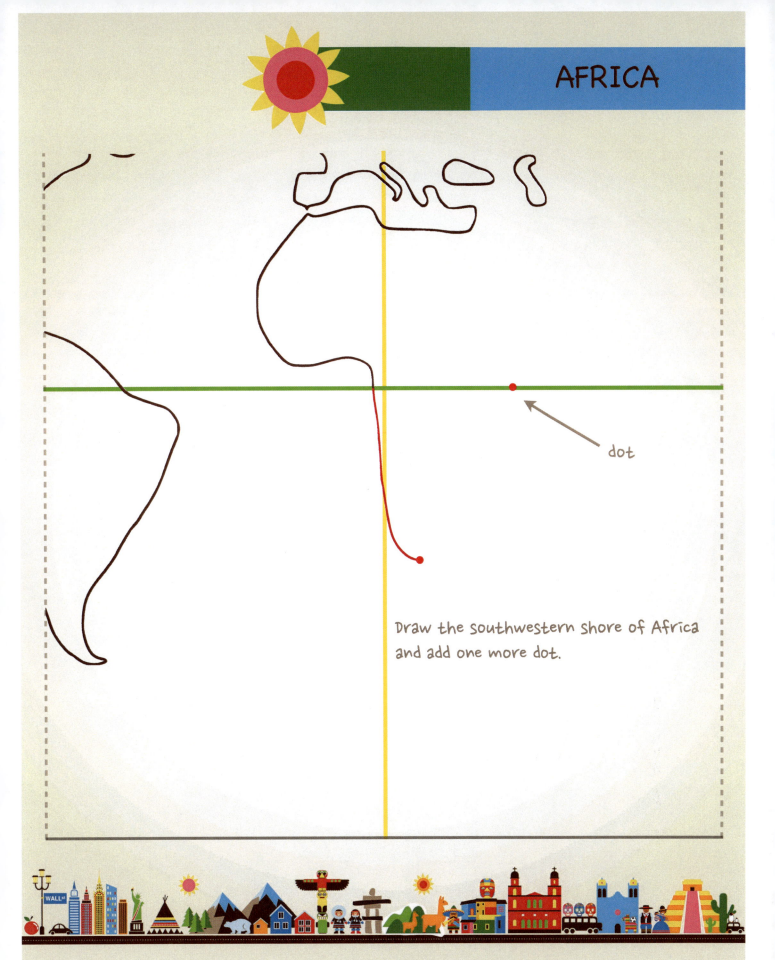

AFRICA

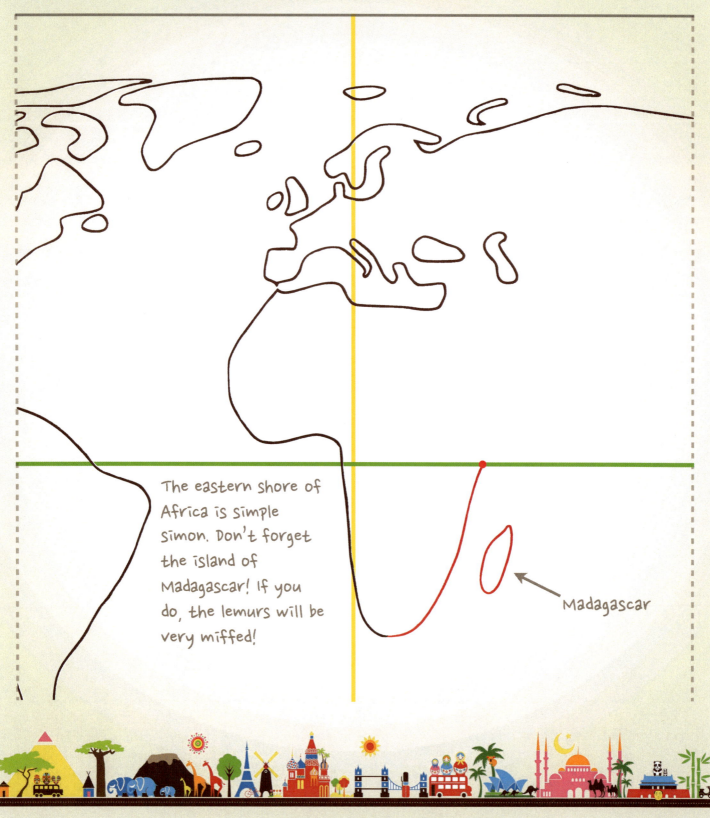

The eastern shore of Africa is simple simon. Don't forget the island of Madagascar! If you do, the lemurs will be very miffed!

Madagascar

AFRICA

horn-like thingy

This last bit of Africa has a horn-like thingy that sticks out to the east. It is a peninsula called, appropriately, the Horn of Africa.

ASIA

Now we will begin the Saudi Arabian peninsula with a tilted "L."

ASIA

dot

To finish the peninsula turn the "L" into a boot. Don't forget to add the dot!

ASIA

Connect the boot to the dot like so. The long triangular peninsula is India and the tiny teardrop is Sri Lanka.

Sri Lanka

ASIA

New Siberian Islands

imaginary halfway mark

Now we will return to northern Asia. Extend the northern shore of Russia into a long fishhook shape like so. Notice that it is quite far north of the imaginary halfway mark.

Add an oval to represent a group of islands called the New Siberian Islands.

ASIA

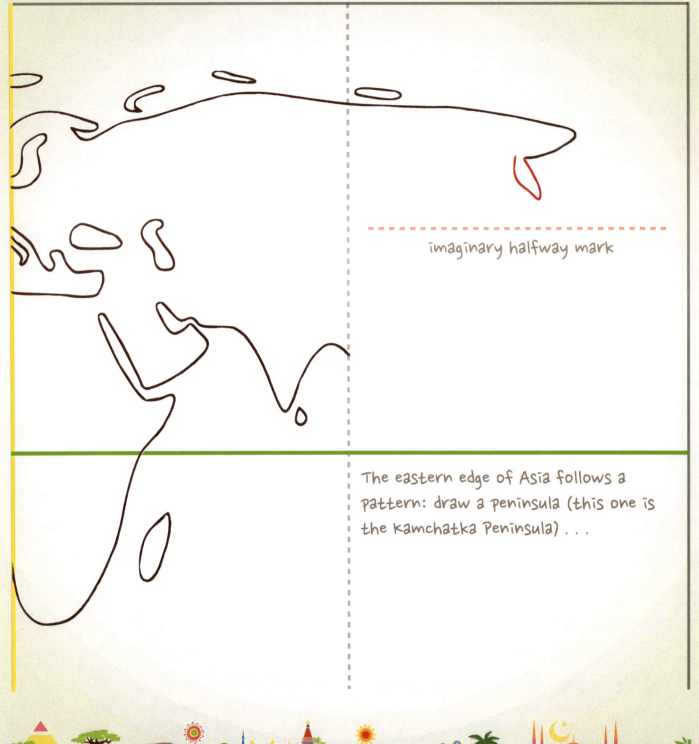

imaginary halfway mark

The eastern edge of Asia follows a pattern: draw a peninsula (this one is the Kamchatka Peninsula)...

 ASIA

...imaginary halfway mark

...then draw an "s"...

ASIA

. . . then another peninsula (this time it is the Koreas) . . .

ASIA

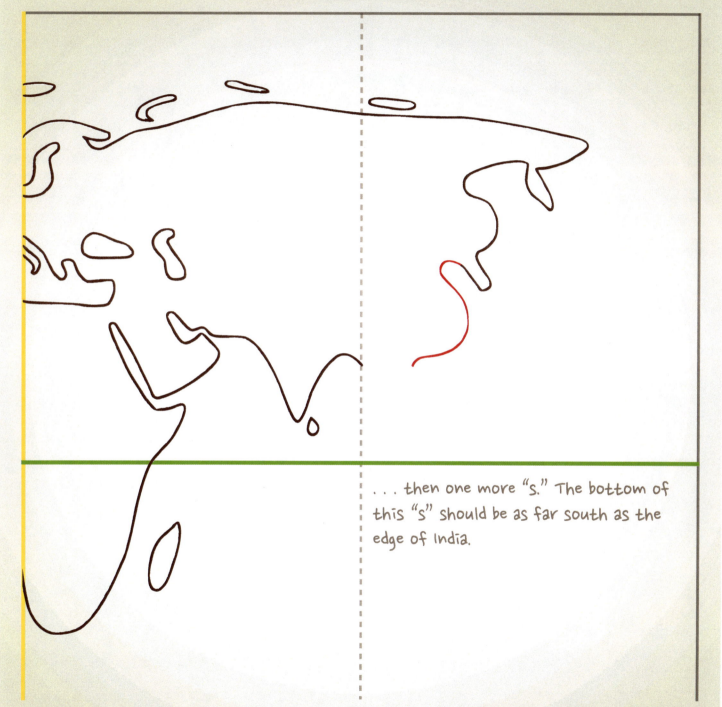

. . . then one more "s." The bottom of this "s" should be as far south as the edge of India.

ASIA

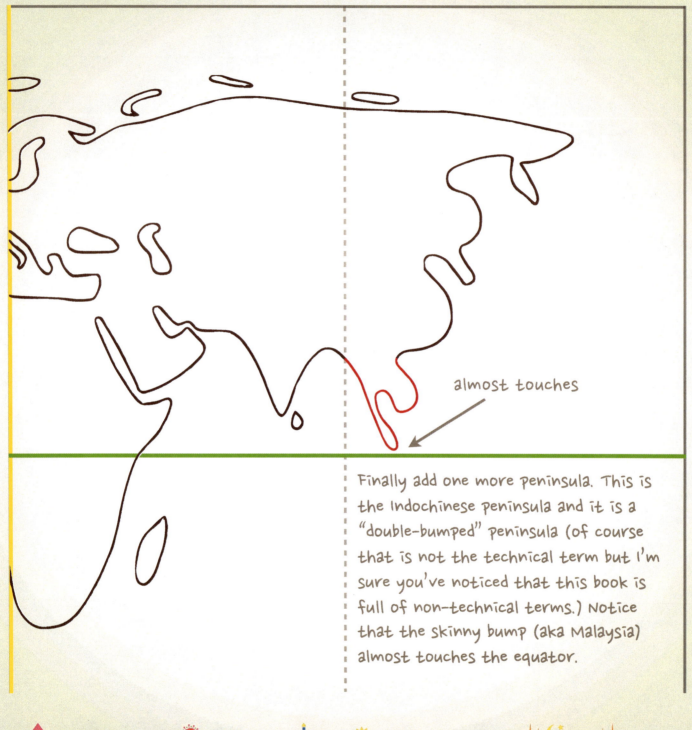

almost touches

Finally add one more peninsula. This is the Indochinese peninsula and it is a "double-bumped" peninsula (of course that is not the technical term but I'm sure you've noticed that this book is full of non-technical terms.) Notice that the skinny bump (aka Malaysia) almost touches the equator.

ASIA

Asia contains many islands. We will represent Japan with just the four major islands. Notice where Japan is located in relation to the Korean peninsula.

ASIA

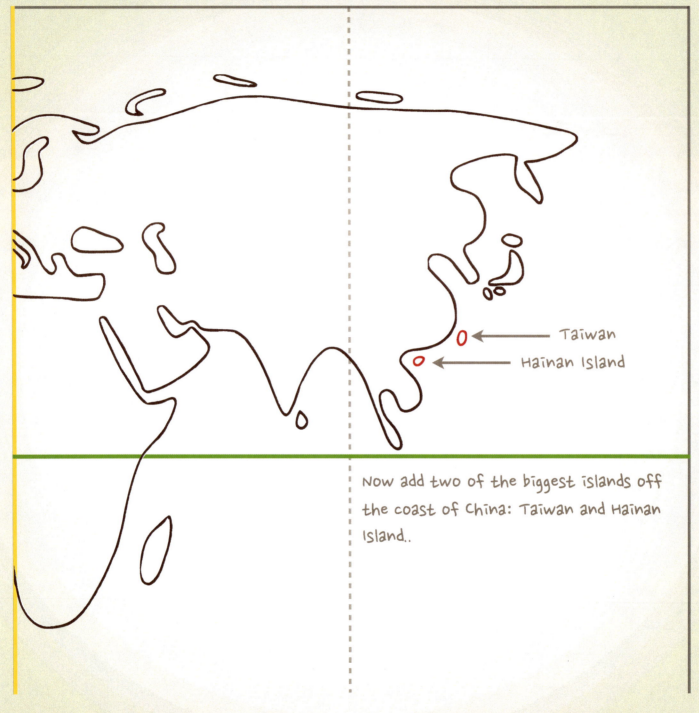

Taiwan
Hainan Island

Now add two of the biggest islands off the coast of China: Taiwan and Hainan Island..

ASIA

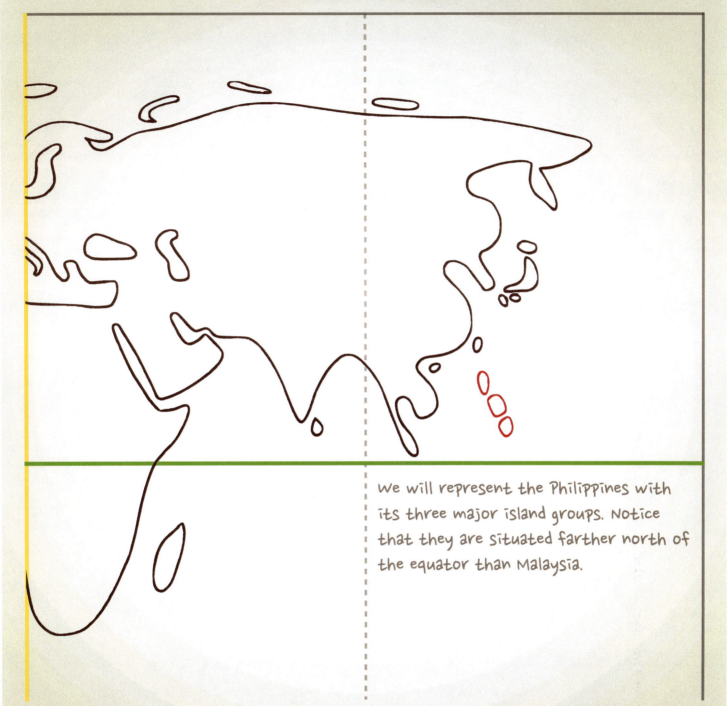

We will represent the Philippines with its three major island groups. Notice that they are situated farther north of the equator than Malaysia.

ASIA

Like Canada, Indonesia is complicated, so we will simplify it by drawing only the five major islands*: Sumatra, Java, Borneo, Sulawesi and New Guinea.**

*Alas, we are, again, leaving out many islands and a few tiny countries. But remember, this is a simplified outline of the world.
**Though we are including New Guinea within Asia, it is important to note that it is technically part of the Australian continent.

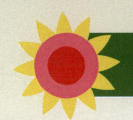 

AUSTRALIA

On to Australia! Notice that it is north of the imaginary halfway mark AND it has a gap at the top.

imaginary halfway mark

AUSTRALIA

Tasmania

- - - - - imaginary halfway mark

Fill in the gap with the Gulf of Carpentaria and add the island of Tasmania. Notice that Tasmania is also north of the imaginary halfway mark.

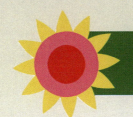 

ZEALANDIA

imaginary halfway mark

New Zealand is considered part of the Australian continent, though technically it is its own microcontinent called Zealandia. Cool!

We are almost finished! Just one continent to go!

ANTARCTICA

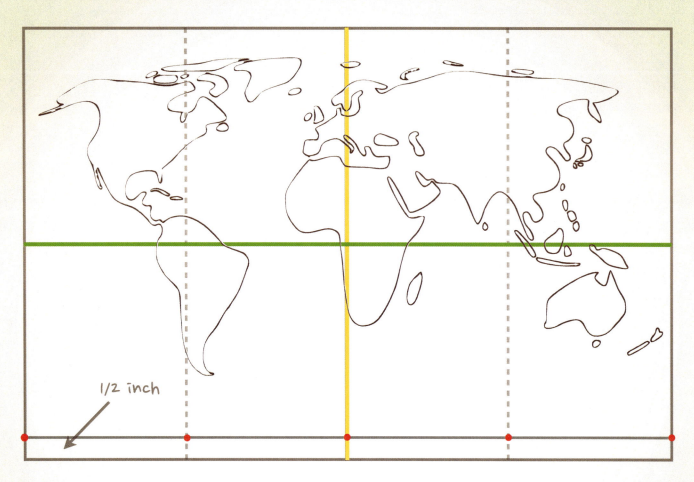

1/2 inch

Before we draw Antarctica we need to draw a border along the bottom of the page. Place a dot 1/2 inch from the bottom as shown above, and then connect the dots. Antarctica will sit above this line and you can label your map with your name and date within the border.

ANTARCTICA

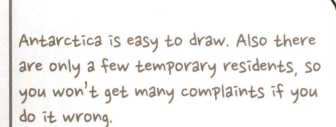

Antarctica is easy to draw. Also there are only a few temporary residents, so you won't get many complaints if you do it wrong.

Begin with this line. The indent is the Ross Ice Shelf.

Ross Ice Shelf

ANTARCTICA

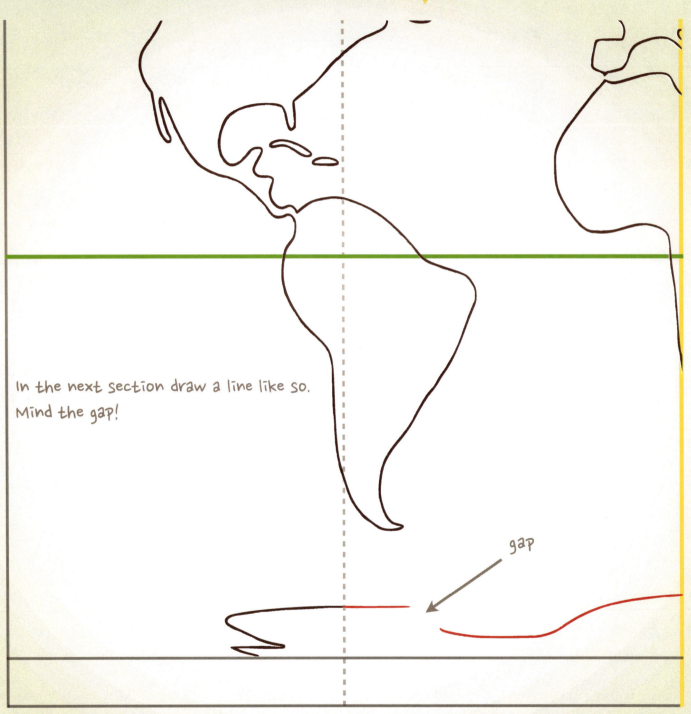

In the next section draw a line like so. Mind the gap!

gap

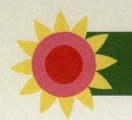

ANTARCTICA

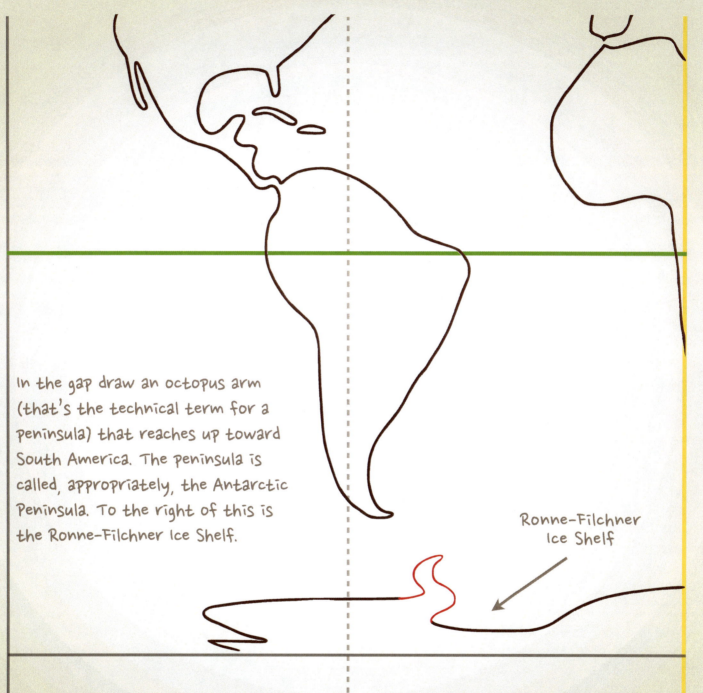

In the gap draw an octopus arm (that's the technical term for a peninsula) that reaches up toward South America. The peninsula is called, appropriately, the Antarctic Peninsula. To the right of this is the Ronne-Filchner Ice Shelf.

Ronne-Filchner Ice Shelf

ANTARCTICA

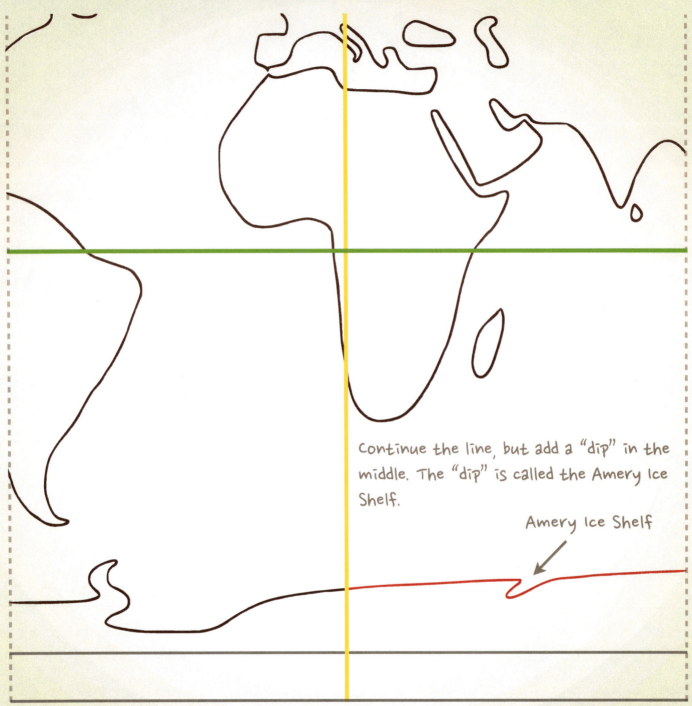

Continue the line, but add a "dip" in the middle. The "dip" is called the Amery Ice Shelf.

Amery Ice Shelf

ANTARCTICA

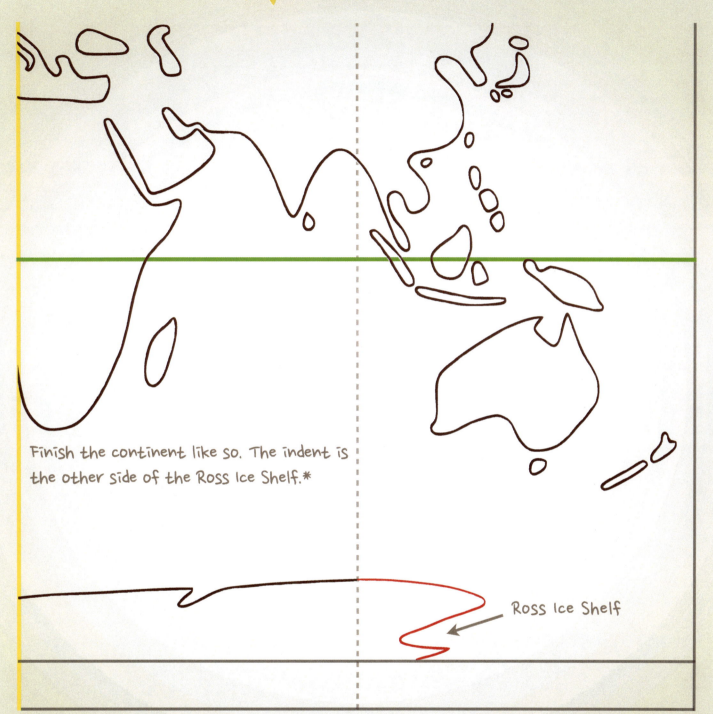

Finish the continent like so. The indent is the other side of the Ross Ice Shelf.*

Ross Ice Shelf

*Remember that Antarctica is a round continent that sits at the bottom of a sphere. It only looks like this when we "unroll" the three-dimensional sphere onto a two-dimensional piece of paper. If you "roll" the sphere back up, the two sides of the Ross Ice Shelf would meet.

THE WORLD

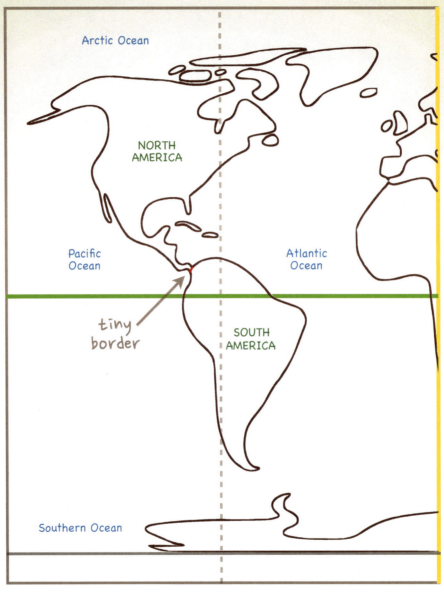

Finally we will mark the borders between continents and add labels. The tiny border between North and South America is easy to draw (but difficult to see).

THE WORLD

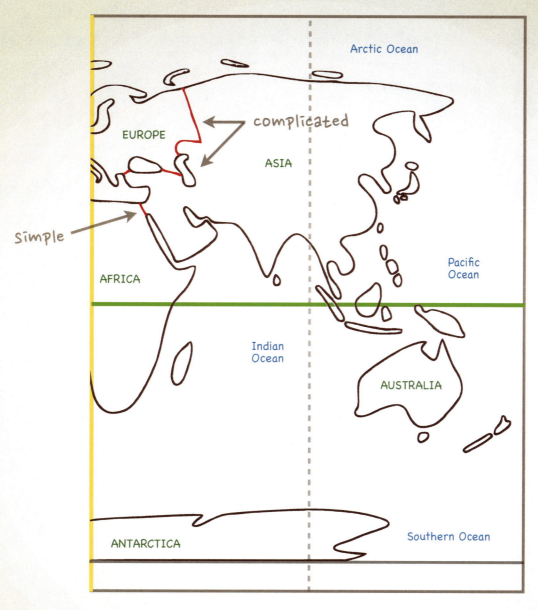

The border between Africa and Asia is simple, but the border between Europe and Asia has three parts and is therefore a little more complicated. Label the rest of the continents and oceans and voila! You're finished!

THE WORLD

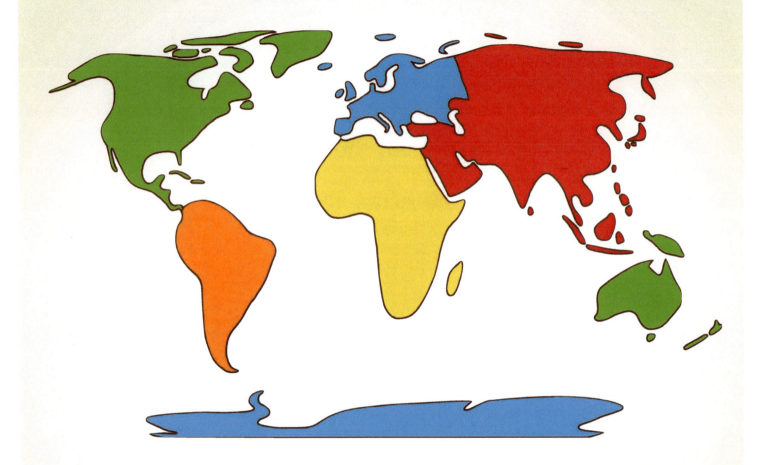

Congratulations!
You can draw the world!

Made in the USA
Monee, IL
04 February 2024